Knock Down Ginger
and other poems

Brian Moses

CAMBRIDGE
UNIVERSITY PRESS

For Anne – with love

Published by the Press Syndicate of the University of Cambridge
The Pitt Building, Trumpington Street, Cambridge CB2 1RP
40 West 20th Street, New York, NY 10011–4211, USA
10 Stamford Road, Oakleigh, Melbourne 3166, Australia

First published 1994

Printed in Great Britain at the University Press, Cambridge

A catalogue record for this book is available from the British Library

Library of Congress cataloguing in publication data applied for

ISBN 0 521 44140 4 hardback
ISBN 0 521 44683 X paperback

Cover and text illustration by Jolyon Webb

Project editor: Claire Llewellyn

Contents

A new beginning

It's always good to make resolutions at New Year, even if you break them very soon afterwards! Have you ever tried striking a bargain with Mum or Dad – "I'll stop doing this, if you'll stop doing that . . ."?

I won't come in late from school, Mum,
if you'll promise to give up smoking.
I'll try not to tease my sister,
she knows I'm only joking.

If you promise not to shout so much,
I'll pick up my clothes at night.
Just don't moan at me all day
and I'll keep away from fights.

Last year's new beginning
didn't last for very long.
I kept my part of the bargain, Mum,
but where did you go wrong?

Those were the days

Sometimes it becomes a little annoying when adults keep starting sentences with "When I was young . . .", particularly if they imply that they were far more virtuous, and behaved far better than children do today! In the last verse of this poem Mum gets the answer she deserves from her child. I have to admit to "stealing" the last two lines from something I overheard in a staff room.

Mum always says she scrimped and saved,
we have it too easy today,
there's nothing we have to work for
and everything comes our way.

"When I was a girl," she says,
"my clothes were hand-me-down.
I had older brothers and sisters,
there wasn't much money around.

"We made our own entertainment,
dressed up or played in the street,
our treats were Saturday pictures
with sixpence to spend on sweets.

"If ever a teacher walloped us,
we wouldn't have dared tell Mum.
'Wait till your Dad gets home,' she'd say,
then he'd have clouted us one."

Oh, those were the days, when you were young, Mum,
long ago before my birth,
when televisions were black and white
and dinosaurs ruled the Earth!

The family book

Knowing something about our roots can give us a sense of identity –
who we are, where we've come from, and the things that have helped
to shape our lives.

My father had a great interest in our family tree, and could trace back
our ancestors for four or five generations. He would always be looking
through old photographs, and once he started pointing things out, I
knew I'd be in for a long session. My father died in 1983 but I think of
'The family book' as his poem.

My father unlocks the family book
where the captured Victorians sit
tight-lipped, keeping their own closed counsel.
I find them caught at christenings
as the greats collect with the latest,
and another name is tied to the family line;
or posed (but not poised) in studios,
the fathers and sons from their Sunday slumbers,
suited and sober and seemingly shy
as if their souls could be stolen away
for the price of a print on paper.

I watch my father separate the great-greats
from the great, the proud patriarchs,
the weddings and unsmiling aunts,
the fishermen released from their nets,
the light keeper and his shiny wife.
I flick back the pages and try to find
my fingerprints in their faces.

Uncle

I don't remember that much about Uncle; I was quite young when he came to stay with us. He was really my great-uncle but we didn't bother with that. I do remember that he smelt of tobacco and that on Sunday mornings he cleaned everyone's shoes.

When I wrote the poem I tried to make cleaning shoes sound really interesting.

Uncle was Gran's brother,
came to stay when she died,
kept to his room at the top of the stairs
but on Sundays he polished shoes.

Uncle was expert, a real shoe sheriff.
Each Size 10 had a price on its head
till he rounded it up with the rest.
He'd lasso Mum's boots and whistle
till plimsolls came running.
He knew, of course, where I threw mine,
when one was missing, he'd corner the dog,
then search through his bed till he found it.

The shoes submitted instantly.
They waited, trembling in line,
while one by one Uncle slapped on polish,
cleaned off the week's wear and tear
then buffed them to a shine.

He'd brighten the shabbiest pair,
the ones that had skulked for months
in a cupboard beneath the stairs.
He'd untangle loops and knots
then leave the shoes in rows
till, like some general inspecting troops,
I'd signal which ones went back
for a second go.

I took on his job when he died,
cleaned shoes for money.
I'd rub away like Aladdin and think
how my efforts might free Uncle's ghost.
I knew how much he'd be missing that mix
of polish and Sunday roast.

Walking in autumn with Grandad

Quite often I'm asked to write poems to order. A letter will arrive to say that poems are needed for an anthology on one subject or another, and I'll start scribbling. This poem was written for such a request, and I wanted to bring to it a number of things that I remembered from holidays in the country when I was a boy.

"There's a change in the air," Grandad says,
"a chill in the breeze, now autumn's come.
You can hear it too, if you listen,
listen to the leaves and their whisperings."

Each evening now he calls and we trek
over the field towards the trees,
where rabbits play in the last of the sun
till Grandad claps his hands and they run for cover.

We collect the seeds from sycamores
and flip them into the air.
He jokes how the spread of leaves on the ground
looks a lot like our front-room carpet,
then points to a squirrel, high in an oak,
and we watch as it gathers acorns
to store in some secret place.

An early gale has uprooted trees,
laid them low, like felled giants.
Grandad climbed them when he was a lad,
he and his mates, agile as monkeys,
till down they shinned to comb the hedge
for cobnuts or late blackberries.

Already new trees have been planted,
sturdy saplings that bend but won't break
if another gale comes thumping through.

Grandad says, "Be off with you, run home
while I take it slow." But I stick to his step
and guide his arm as he carefully climbs the stile.
It wouldn't take much to knock *him* down,
now winter looks over his shoulder
and winds are poised to return.

Christmas Day

I wanted to describe a typical Christmas Day in the late 1950s. A very simple structure holds this poem together – each new idea begins with "It was . . .".

It was waking early and making a din.
It was knowing that for the next twenty minutes
    I'd never be quite so excited again.
It was singing the last verse of
    "O Come All Ye Faithful", the one that's
    only meant to be sung on Christmas Day.
It was lighting a fire in the unused room
    and a draught that blew back woodsmoke
    into our faces.
It was lunch and a full table,
    and Dad repeating how he'd once eaten his
    off the bonnet of a lorry in Austria.
It was keeping quiet for the Queen
    and Gran telling that one about children
    being seen but not heard.
    (As if we could get a word in edgeways
    once she started!)
It was Monopoly and me out to cheat the devil
    to be the first to reach Mayfair.
It was "Just a small one for the lad,"
    and Dad saying, "We don't want him getting tiddly."
It was aunts assaulting the black piano
    and me keeping clear of mistletoe
    in case they trapped me.
It was pinning a tail on the donkey,
    and nuts that wouldn't crack
    and crackers that pulled apart but didn't bang.

And then when the day was almost gone,
it was Dad on the stairs,
　　on his way to bed,
　　and one of us saying,
　　"You've forgotten to take your hat off . . ."
　　And the purple or pink or orange paper
　　still crowning his head.

Lovey-dovey

Are you ever embarrassed by your parents? Do they sometimes behave in a ridiculous way? Do you long to tell them to act their age?

This poem grew from the words "lovey-dovey", which I noticed written on a classroom blackboard once – along with other alternatives for the word "nice".

When Dad and Mum go all lovey-dovey
we just don't know where to look.
My sister says, "Cut it out you two,"
while I stick my nose in a book.

Mum has this faraway look on her face
while Dad has a silly grin.
"You don't have to mind us, kids," he says.
We just wish they'd pack it in.

Dad calls Mum, "Little Sugarplum"
and Mum says, "You handsome brute".
Dad laughs and says, "Look at your Mum,
don't you think that she's cute?

"I guess that's why I married her,
she's my truly wonderful one."
Mum says he doesn't mean any of it
but she thinks he's a lot of fun.

I just can't stand all the kissing,
at their age they ought to know better.
I think I'll go up to my room
and write *Jim'll Fix It* a letter.

I hate it when they're lovey-dovey
but I hate it more when they fight
when faces redden and tempers flare
and sharp words cut through the night.

I'd rather they kissed and cuddled
and joked about and laughed,
at least we can tell everything's okay
when Mum and Dad are daft.

Face-pulling contests

How many times have you sat across the table from someone and pulled faces at each other? My daughter and I were doing just that on one occasion and it started me thinking.

My sister and I
hold face-pulling contests.

I start with my
zombie-at-midnight look
while she hooks two fingers
into her mouth and pulls out
her sabre-tooth-tiger scowl.

I try my curse-
of-the-killer-mummies,
but she rolls her eyes
and curls her lip,
sticks out her teeth
and pretends she's Drac.
I clutch at my throat
and finger a bolt,
then zap her with
Frankenstein's features.

She comes at me
with her wolf-woman sneer,
but I can howl
much better than her.
And now she's stuck
for something to do,
and this time I'm thinking
I'll beat her for sure
with my purple-planet-people-eater –

when Mum steps in
to check the noise,
and no one pulls a better face
than Mum when she's annoyed.
My sister and I
are mere beginners –
Mum's the winner!

The g-g-g-g-g-g-g-g-ghost train

A while ago I was asked to write some spooky poems and I thought back to my first trip on a ghost train and remembered how scared I'd been. When we are really frightened of something our voice starts to stutter, and I tried to bring this sensation into the poem with the repetition of the line "On the g-g-g-g-g-g-g-g-ghost train".

This poem is a lot of fun to read aloud. I say it quickly so that the words almost tumble over each other in an effort to escape. I like everyone to join in with "On the g-g-g-g-g-g-g-g-ghost train".

On the g-g-g-g-g-g-g-g-ghost train,
it was dark, it was scary, it was insane,
and I'm never going back there ever again
on the g-g-g-g-g-g-g-g-ghost train.

"It's a lot of fun," my big sister said,
"skeletons, ghosts and a man with his head
tucked under his arm, but you needn't look,
I've been here before." So I sat and I shook

on the g-g-g-g-g-g-g-g-ghost train.

I didn't like it, not one bit,
webs hung down from the ceiling and hit
the side of your face as you travelled past
ever so slowly – oh can't we go fast? –

on the g-g-g-g-g-g-g-g-ghost train.

Coffin lids creaked and a skeleton fell
across our path and I let out a yell
and its echo bounced round the tunnel and back
like a scream from a raving maniac

on the g-g-g-g-g-g-g-g-ghost train.

Back in the open I staggered away.
My sister said, "Maybe another day . . ."
but no, no way could I ever face
another trip through that terrible place

on the g-g-g-g-g-g-g-g-ghost train.
It was dark, it was scary, it was insane,
and I'm never going back there ever again
on the g-g-g-g-g-g-g-g-ghost train.

The ghoul school bus

One morning in December I was out on the road very early. It was still dark and I was driving behind a black bus. I noticed that the windows had shaded glass, so that the people inside the bus couldn't be seen. This seemed somewhat mysterious, perhaps a little spooky.

I usually try and read this poem fairly quietly with a hint of menace in my voice.

The ghoul school bus
is picking up its cargo
of little horrors.

They must all be home
before first light, when today
turns into tomorrow.

All the sons and daughters of vampires,
little Igors and junior Fangs,
the teenage ghouls with their ghoulfriends
all wail, as the bus bell clangs.

And the driver doesn't look well,
he's robed completely in black,
and the signboard says – "Transylvania
by way of hell and back".

The seats are slimy and wet,
there's a terrible graveyard smell,
all the small ghouls cackle and spit,
and practise their ghoulish spells.

The witches are reading their ABCs,
cackling over "D" for disease,
while tomboy zombies are falling apart
and werewolves are checking for fleas.

When the bus slows down to drop them off
at Coffin Corner or Cemetery Gates,
their *mummies* are waiting to greet them
with eyes full of anguish and hate.

The ghoul school bus
is dropping off its cargo
of little horrors.

They must all be home
before first light, when today
turns into tomorrow.

The north face

In this poem I liked the idea of linking the inhospitable and unwelcoming north face of a mountain with the kind of teacher that I sometimes met in my childhood and sometimes still do meet on my visits to schools!

This is the famous north face of our teacher
that's never been known to crack a smile.

This is the famous north face of our teacher,
few have scaled the heights to please her.

Some of us have tried and failed,
some of us knew we hadn't a hope,
some of us were brushed aside
or slid back down the slippery slope.

Not for her any creature comforts,
not for her any softening smile,
only the bleak and icy wastes
of her glacial grimace.

This is the famous north face of our teacher,
all signs of weakness displease her.

But when our Head Teacher wanders in
and says what lovely work we've done,
there's a glimmer of something
that plays on her lips
like a hint of sun between mountains,
only to vanish again
when she starts to speak.

Learning to swim

This poem focuses on an unpleasant episode in my childhood. I have this brutal teacher to thank for my fear of water and my stubborn refusal to learn to swim even now!

Six weeks to learn to swim.
Six weeks and each time our turn came,
it rained or the wind blew,
whipping up waves on the open pool,
strong enough to sink battleships.
No way that I could stay afloat.
I tried my best but my teacher snarled,
"Fingers away from the edge,
I don't want to say it again."
And if I persisted, his foot
would lay over my hand
like the touch of a butterfly,
till suddenly he'd press down hard
and I'd yell and let go.
And the water would flow
into my mouth and up my nose,
and I'd scream an underwater scream,
then surface, gasp and wheeze,
while all the while it seemed
I'd breathed my last.
He claimed each year that everyone swam
by the time they left his class,
but I beat him . . .
I didn't.

Our teacher

Before I became a full-time writer I used to teach. I'd always be telling my classes that they annoyed me, but in this poem I turned the spotlight on myself!

Our teacher taps his toes,
keeping the beat to some silent tune
only he knows.

Our teacher drums his fingers
on his desk, on the window,
on anything, when the room is quiet,
when we're meant to be writing
in silence.

Our teacher cracks his knuckles,
clicks his fingers, grinds his teeth,
his knees are knocking the edge of his desk,
he breathes to a rhythmical beat.

When he turns his head in a certain way
there's a bone that cracks in his neck.
When he sinks to the floor
we often think he'll stay on his knees
for ever more, he's such a physical wreck!

Our teacher bangs his head against the wall
(or pretends to) when someone comes up
with another dumb remark.

Our teacher says we annoy him
with all our silly fuss.
Perhaps he's never really thought
how much he irritates us.

Windy playground

This is another poem which dates back to my time as a teacher. When I was on playground duty I liked to watch children playing and listen in to their games. I wrote this poem after playground duty on a very windy day.

They played blow-me-down in the yard,
letting the wind bully them,
coats above heads, arms spread wide,
daring the wind to do its worst.
They leant forward against the blow
as it rallied and flung them back,
then coats puffed out like clouds
they returned to attack the blast,
while the gale drew a breath and then
pressed relentless. Till wild in defeat
and magnificent, they grouped again
and stretched their wings, stubborn
as early airmen.

Distributing the harvest

This is a true account of the harvest ritual that took place annually at a school where I once taught. For days before the event, all kinds of harvest produce was brought to school and set out in a colourful display – this is the "tableau" in the poem's first line. Once the harvest festival was over, the food was distributed to residents in the town.

Whose point of view do you think the poem represents – the pupils' or their teacher's?

We collapsed the tableau carefully,
passing it piece by piece to a class
of kids, arms held up to make their bids
for brussels, for solid and sensible spuds
to ballast the base of baskets.
The eggs looked on from safe distance
while tomatoes split their skins and sticky
apples slipped and rolled across the polished floor,
to be challenged and captured and pushed
into bags, now swollen fat with harvest swag,
until all that remained were laidback marrows,
stout heroes of the garden patch.

Then burdens were lifted, shouldered and
shifted, till like some desert caravan of
Oriental kings with gifts, our harvest bearers
struggled out, towards the town, across the bridge.
Later we heard of casualties, someone's
cucumber spun under a car, while others on
the farthest run found no one home and hauled
it back or posted produce through letter flaps;
but then we knew nothing of that.
We heard instead, all afternoon, news of
successful missions and watched returning faces,
bright as harvest moons.

Classroom globe

This is another poem based on a true incident at a school where I
taught. Each child reacted to our globe, many treating it as a play
thing, but Jenny's gesture meant something different.

We strung our globe from the rafters
then watched how the continents spun.
We were dizzy with faraway places,
they swam before our eyes.
Everyone wanted to take a swipe at
the planet, to roll the world, to cause
global chaos. We laughed at the
notion of some great hand, sweeping down
avalanches, rolling earthquakes round
Africa, knocking elephants off their feet.
Then reasons were found for leaving seats,
to touch, or tilt, or hit heads on the planet,
squaring up to the world like March hares.
We talked of how the Earth had been damaged,
leaving it bruised, sore from neglect,
and Jenny, who feels sorry for anyone and
anything, leant her brow against the planet
and felt the sorrow and pain of Earth
in a cold hard globe.

Whale

I have always been fascinated by whales. I was once promised a
sighting of whales on a ferry trip off Western Canada, and then was
very disappointed when nothing showed up.

This poem imagines a time when whales are on the brink of extinction
and specimens are being killed for display in museums.

In this room, and the next, and the next,
you will see a whale; huge creatures once found
in all oceans of the world,
criss-crossing the waters,
sending signals we failed to hear.
Till whales all but disappeared,
and then it was far too late.

We chased this one for several days,
repaired the damage the harpoon made,
and now this specimen is as good as new.
This was the one they called "Big Blue".

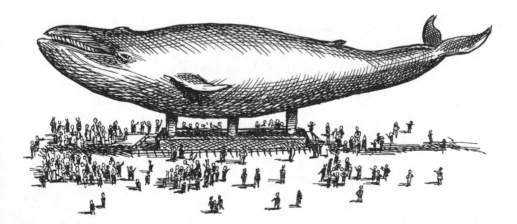

Names

I suppose there is a certain kind of humour in this poem, but it is a black humour to match the bleak mood I was in when I wrote it.

I feel very concerned about the continued mistreatment of our environment, and at the time of writing this poem, world leaders were gathering for yet another conference about the future of our planet. As I listened to the news reports of arguments and disagreements, I began to feel that we couldn't hope for much of a future.

My name is "Couldn't care less",
just let the forests die.
My name is "Can't be bothered",
who cares about holes in the sky?

My name is "I'm too busy",
let someone else do the worrying,
there's nothing that I can do
if the ice caps are wearing thin.

My name is "Leave me alone",
just don't go preaching to me.
Gossip is what I care about
not oil that's spilt in the sea.

My name is "I'm all right Jack",
there's really no cause for alarm.
Hens are silly birds, who cares
if they suffer at the factory farm?

Who cares about global warming?
I like a spot of hot weather.
My name is "Sit on the fence",
my name is "All of a dither".

So stop saying what I should think,
I don't want to believe what I'm told.
My name is "Hope it will go away",
my name is "Don't get involved".

And who do you think you are,
telling us all we should worry?
WELL, MY NAME'S A WARNING FROM FUTURE YEARS,
IT'S "LISTEN OR YOU'LL BE SORRY".

The beach donkeys

A Welsh poet, Dylan Thomas, once wrote that the memories of our childhood have no order and no end, and for me that's true. I'm always finding that places I visit or things people say can trigger off memories of when I was a child.

I came across some donkeys in their winter quarters one year, and this was just the trigger I needed to start me writing.

Led from fields and hastily fed,
then bunched into fours and roughly harnessed,
Neddy to Dolly, Mickey to Joe,
bridles set between teeth, straps pulled hard
across flanks and buckled beneath.

We laughed and pointed and patted the donkeys,
or heard the clip-clop and ran to stare
at the silly shaggy creatures,
jammed against cars at the lights,
till the traffic unscrambled itself
and a crack of command shifted the teams.

In heavy heat they treadmilled sand
while the fierce sun branded their backs
and tricky cargoes tugged at the reins:
sticky kids and lovers and stout grans
waving at cameras, and candyfloss girls
with their mums, and the kiss-me-quick
comedians who struggled and bumped along.

All day the donkeys trekked and turned,
were fed with ices and flat-handed sweets
till their tired riders abandoned the beach.
Then hooked to staging posts they stood
with the spent deckchairs and the debris
of fine weather, while masters counted
the takings and waited for paid lads
to clip the beasts and race them home
down suddenly sunless streets.

Fishing summer

In the seaside town where I grew up there were always people fishing from the harbour wall. I loved to watch them with the mess of equipment and bait at their feet. Soon I had my own rod and learnt that the best time to fish was when the tide had turned and was heading back to the shore, bringing fish to feed on creatures that lived in the lee of the harbour wall.

I remember fishing every day for two summers, and have tried to show something of my fascination for the sport in this poem.

Mandy and I were fishing companions
rushing to catch the tide before it turned,
our tackle spilling from saddlebags, our
pockets crammed with fat paper wallets of
fresh dug lug. And casting we'd encounter
familiar hazards, reels spun at our first
attempts, lines tangled and sprouted birds' nests;
we spent precious time unravelling till
tides turned and the fish bit fast. We caught an
old lag of a crab that came up fighting.
It bubbled and spat with vicious claws splayed
out like a baseball catcher, then edged off
sideways across the pier to drop-plop down
to the water beneath. There were rumours too
of some dreadful beasts that slithered from clefts
in search of food, of monster congers that
wrapped their tails round rocks and then gave battle.
There were times when we wished the big fish would
bite, though we doubted the strength of our lines.
We'd visualise fantastic catches,
our photos in angling magazines, but
nothing that size ever gobbled our bait.

Mandy and I were fishing companions
packing away with the last of the light
before slinking home along alleyways
while darkness spread its nets all over town.

Knock down ginger

Most children have played this game at some time and in one form or another. On the Isle of Wight it's called "Ginger knocking", in Guernsey it's "Knock and run". You may call it something different but basically it involves knocking on a door and then running away before you're spotted.

I often feel the need to "confess" to my childhood misdeeds in my poems. I played in the street from an early age and learnt that my view of fun wasn't always shared by other people!

There was only one game that we wanted to play
when we met each day to discuss our plans.
It was "Knock down ginger", all round the streets,
till shrinking from sight behind parked cars
we'd hear our latest victim yelling,
"I know you, I know your Dad!"

"She does, too," someone would say. "She'll give him
an earful, no doubt about that."
And then if we felt like dangerous living
we'd do it again, till maddened with rage
she'd burst from her house and tear up the road.
Like a mad bull looking for someone to gore,
she'd rat-a-tat-tat on all of our doors.

We'd set ourselves tasks – "Can you scoot
up that path, ring the bell, then scoot back down
before they can tell who it is?"
There were accidents, too, in our haste to escape.
Pete knocked ladders into a hedge, while Les
backed away into somebody's pond, then skittled
a dozen gnomes as he splashed his way out.

Then one day, down a different street,
we knocked on a door and no one came – no threats,
no movement. We half crept out
and heard the sound of bolts pulled back
and a key being turned in the lock.
Something held us there and stopped us tearing away
as we usually did till a voice, still hidden
behind the door, crackled out, "I'm coming, I'm
coming."

She must have been about ninety-eight, frail, shaky –
it would have taken all her strength to struggle up –
we couldn't just disappear. We helped her in
and found her chair, put the kettle on for tea.
"We're sorry," we said, "we knocked at your door."
She said she was glad and that no one else
had called for a week, maybe more. "We'll call again,"
we said, and at that moment, believed we would.

We didn't, of course, but after that we were
pretty good for a week or two, till we found
new ways to have some fun,
annoying the neighbourhood!

Excavations

Some time ago the road outside my house was being dug up so that new gas pipes could be installed. It was winter, and the work took weeks to complete. I watched the workmen and their machines in all kinds of weather. At the weekend I watched the local kids enjoying the mud. I made some notes about what I saw and later used them in this poem.

Big machines are digging in the road,
gulping up great gobfuls of mud
then swinging it round to sling it out
or shoot it clump by clump into trucks.

For street kids propped up by bikes
these loads hold a fascination,
odd machines huff-puffing up slopes,
their actions somehow satisfying.

At the busy weekend they are stilled,
inconveniently parked on heaps
of clay, half-obstructing entranceways,
while kids scale ridges of mini-
mountains, suction tugging their boots.

But on grim, dim days of puddles
and rain, while men balance pipes on backs
before pitching them into ditches,
the scene resembles those sepia snaps
where soldiers, strung-out along skylines,
slid-marched across boards, their rifles
shoulder-high so they shouldn't be
dropped or blocked by mud.

And at night a lonely light like
some substitute moon, reveals a
landscape not unlike those lunar
TV pictures beamed from space,
with traces of tracks in the dirt,
as if these buggies had worked
their way through moondust.

Readathon-sleepathon

"Readathon" is an annual event in which schools can take part. The idea is to read as many books as possible over a set period of time. Sponsors then donate money according to how many books have been read. This is then sent to an appeal for children with cancer.

I was asked to read some of my poems to 170 girls who were holding a "Sleepathon". The girls turned up for school on Friday, with their sleeping bags, nightwear, teddy bears and piles of books to read. They then "camped out" in the school hall on Friday night and went home on Saturday morning.

This poem is dedicated to the pupils and staff who took part in the "Readathon-sleepathon" at Rainham High School for Girls in November 1990.

Mary is sleeping by Janice, and Janice is next to Louise,
and Louise is squeezed beside Tracy who's pressed
      against Alice's knees.
And Sally is pally with Gemma, and Gemma is talking
      with Claire,
and Claire is thinking that maybe she should have stayed
      home and washed her hair –

but it's the readathon-sleepathon,
a ghosts-at-midnight screamathon,
and anyone who's anyone
is reading at the readathon.

But Ann-Marie would dearly love to be at home in bed,
lying safely in her room while silence fills her head,
and Nicola is tired and would like to get to sleep
but all that talk of ghosts has given her the creeps.

And "I need to go to the toilet, Miss, I'm not going on
    my own,
someone had better come with me, it's not like being at
    home."
"Hey, come and give me a kiss, Miss, my Mum always
    does,
and tuck me up really tight, Miss, go on, make a fuss – "

at the dramathon, the pyjamathon,
I'd rather run a marathon,
but anyone who's anyone
is reading at the readathon.

It's been going on for 19 hours and it's been a lot
    of fun,
but now it's early morning and someone wants her Mum.
In just a few more hours we can all creep home to bed,
dream of money raised and the number of books we've
    read –

at the readathon, the pleadathon,
the money-for-people-in-needathon,
and anyone who's anyone
is reading at the readathon.

And then when it's finally over and everything's cleared
    from the floor,
when everyone's saying goodbye and heading for the door
it's a readathon, stampedathon,
a mega-brill succeedathon,
a guaranteed repeatathon –
will you be here next year?

The cowpat-throwing contest

Cowpat-throwing contests are still held in North America, but a
hundred years or so ago they used to be much more popular. Cowboys
used to drive cattle across country to market, then once the cows were
sold, they liked to relax and have fun. They would start with a few
beers in the saloon and then hold various contests. Cowpat-throwing
often proved the highlight of the day's activities.

In this poem I imagined three lads hearing about this wonderful pursuit
and trying it out for themselves.

Malc and me and Ian Grey, we couldn't believe
when we heard someone say, that in cattle towns
of the old Wild West, they held cowpat-throwing contests!

How awful, how dreadful, what if it hit
you smack in the mouth, you'd gag, you'd be sick,
but we knew, even then, the day would come when we'd
    try it.

And it wasn't very long after that when the three of us
were sent away – "Get out of the house,
get out of my sight, go somewhere else and play."

And we walked until the houses stopped, looked
over a hedge and there in a field were pancakes of
the very stuff we'd been talking about for days.

The cows looked friendly so we started up
with a chunk or two that might have been mud
but we knew we'd move on to the slimy stuff before long.

Malc was the first to try it out and scooped up
a really terrible lump, but while Ian was yelling
and backing away, he tripped and sat down in the dung.

Malc was laughing fit to burst and he must have forgotten
his hands were full till he dropped the lot
all down his trousers, then wiped his hands on his shirt.

I made the mistake of grinning too till Malc hit my jacket
and Ian my shoes, and I watched it spreading everywhere,
while the cows just stood there and mooed!

Well, after that it was in our hair and down our jumpers
and everywhere. Our fingernails were full of the stuff,
then Ian said, "Pax, I've had enough."

"We look awful," Malc said, "and we smell as sweet as
a sewage farm in the midday heat. We shouldn't have
   done it,
we've been really daft" – but again Ian started to laugh.

We laughed up the lane while a cloud of flies
trailed us back to Ian's place, where his Mum's grim face
soon shut us up, as she fixed her hose to the tap.

"It's history, Mum, it's really true. It's what they did
in the Wild West – " but we lost the rest of what he said
as a jet of water pounded his chest.

Then water was turned on Malc and me, and we both went home
in Ian's clothes, while his Mum phoned ours and tried
to explain just what it was that we'd done.

I knew my Mum would have a fit. "That's it,"
she said, "the final straw. No way you're going out
to play for a week, no, a month, maybe more.

"Get in that bath, use plenty of soap, how could you be
such a silly dope? Use the nailbrush too and wash
your hair. I'll be in there later to check."

I scrubbed and I brushed but I couldn't make the smell
disappear, and I wondered how the cowboys coped
when their contest was done and everyone climbed in
the tub.

And kids held their noses and called out, "Pooh!"
for days and weeks and months after that, but it didn't
matter,
we'd proved we were best, not at spellings or sport
or school reports, but at cowpat-throwing contests.

Kiss chase

A girl in a school I once visited remarked that I didn't write many
poems from a girl's point of view. I admitted that a lot of my poems
were autobiographical – about my own life and childhood, and that I
wrote through the eyes of a young boy. I promised that I'd try to write
some poems about girls' concerns. "What would you like me to write
about?" I asked. "Kiss chase," she answered.

I don't play kiss chase with boys any more,
they're rough and they're trouble,
they take it too far.
They pester and push and they're rowdy too,
thinking that all they've got to do
is to corner you somewhere, where nobody sees,
and you'll melt and submit and say, "Oh yes, please!"
But half of the lads never clean their teeth,
and I don't want to find out what lies beneath
those crumbling rocks that guard their mouths,
so I belt them one – you should hear them howl!
Now they won't play kiss chase with me any more,
they say I'm too rough and I take it too far.
So all in all it's worked out okay,
but the odd thing is there's a lad called Ben,
and I really would like to play
kiss chase with him,
but he won't.

Soft centre

I remember how terribly hard it used to be to pretend that I was the strong and silent type. I hated the pretence, and it kept me apart from people I would have liked to be with. Why did I do it? – because I was part of a gang, and my loyalty to the gang was stronger than my desire to break free. But, oh, the torment . . .

I pull her hair,
call out names,
join in all of
my mates' rough games.

I swagger past
as she looks my way,
strong and silent,
nothing to say.

I mess about,
make out I'm tough,
but underneath
I'm soft enough.

And really I'd like
to hold her tight,
pause for a while
beneath streetlights,

buy her coffee,
talk until late,
kiss goodnight,
tell her she's great.

But I'm meeting my mates
at the club tonight.
I couldn't do it,
it wouldn't be right.

So she smiles
and I scowl,
she speaks
and I growl.

Have fun with words

Now that you have read some of my poems, I'm hoping that they might spark off some ideas for your own writing. You may also like to try out some of the ideas I've suggested in this next part of the book. Not every poem has an activity to go with it. The poems I've used for activities are the ones that I have read in schools and which seem to get people talking!

When you start to plan some writing of your own, think about things that have happened to you – somewhere you've visited, perhaps, or something that has happened at school. Look around you and listen to what people say. Is there something memorable there? Sounds, sights, smells, tastes, the feel of something – ideas are everywhere and available to everyone.

Try working with a friend or two, and sharing ideas. Everyone will have something different to say about families, holidays, pets, games, school, food and all the other areas of everyday life. Talk about what you are going to write, jot down ideas, and then decide on the best.

When you are ready to begin putting ideas down on paper, don't worry about making mistakes. Write things down in any order you like. You may find that ideas come so quickly you have to write really fast. If you don't know how to spell a word, don't worry about it now, write it down as you think. It is much better to use a word you like than settle for one you're not really happy with. Experiment with your writing. Try putting words in a different order, or arranging them to make a pattern on the page. Then read what you have written to others – but maybe practise it first.

Have fun with words. I always do.

"A new beginning" (p. 5)

Try thinking of a list of bargains that you might make with members of your family. If Dad stops going on about how great pop music was in his day, then you'll turn down your CD player; if your sister stops bossing you about, then you'll stop embarrassing her in front of her friends – and so on.

Alternatively, you could try thinking up a list of the things you enjoy doing but which your parents disapprove of – like watching television, seeing your best friend every day, or going swimming five times a week. Then write another list of the things your parents try and make you do, but which you hate – eat fish, go on long walks, tidy your room, and so on. Can you bring these ideas together in a poem? Lists can sometimes be inspiring!

> I always enjoy watching television,
> but you always tell me it's bad for my eyes.
> I always hate eating cabbage,
> but you always say that it's good for me.
> I always . . .

"The family book" (p. 7), "Uncle" (p. 8) and "Walking in autumn with Grandad" (p. 10)

It can be interesting to write about relatives, but you have to be careful what you say! Small details bring people to life. In my family, for example, Uncle polished shoes, Grandma was pushed round town in a bathchair, and Aunt Alice kept a parrot.

If I wanted to write about my Aunt Alice, I would begin by making notes:
– Aunt Alice wore a black mac, even in summer.
– She always talked about rain.
– Her parrot had a wicked beak, shaped like a scimitar.
– If the parrot squawked too much, she covered its cage.
– She longjohnsilvered her way round the room. (Yes, I

know Long John Silver is a name, but I'm experimenting and using it as a verb – you can get away with this in poetry!)

Once the notes were complete, I'd start linking up words and phrases that might form part of the poem.

Alice's parrot

Aunt Alice wore a black mac
in the heat of summer,
and talked of rain
on the sunniest of days.

She longjohnsilvered
her way round the room
while her parrot swore,
then nibbled her ear.

There are plenty of poems about families. You might like to look at some of them in *You Just Can't Win*, edited by Brian Moses (Blackie) and *Meet My Folks* by Ted Hughes (Faber).

"Christmas Day" (p. 12)

This poem is rather like a collage. Small fragments of memory are joined together and gradually build up a picture of a typical Christmas Day in the late 1950s. The same two words – "It was . . ." – are the starting point for each new idea.

If you try to write in this way yourself, take care to make each idea as interesting as you can. It is easy to write a long list of items but forget to concentrate on the quality of expression in each idea. For example, with a little more thought, "Christmas is a time for joy" might become "Christmas is a time for joy, happiness and wet kisses under the mistletoe."

"Lovey-dovey" (p. 14)

Can you think of other words like lovey-dovey that sound the same and are linked by a hyphen? What about itsy-bitsy or hurly-burly? Can you use one as the title of a poem?

Hurly-burly

There's a hurly-burly in our house,
it happens first thing each day
when we all charge into the bathroom
and get in each other's way! . . .

Other verses might describe a hurly-burly at school, a football match, or in the bus queue, and so on.

"The g-g-g-g-g-g-g-g-ghost train" (p. 18)

Fairgrounds may give you lots of ideas for writing. Which is your favourite, or least favourite, ride? You could try piling up words and rhymes and reading them at a breathless pace:

On the roller-coaster,
hold tight round the bend,
on the roller-coaster,
will this journey never end?
On the roller-coaster,
sit tight for the hill,
on the roller-coaster,
I'm feeling ill . . .

Out of breath
on the Wall of Death.
Hitchin' a ride
on the astro-slide.
Hear them squeal
at the top of the wheel.
Lost for days
in the giant maze.

"The ghoul school bus" (p. 20)

With a friend, write about some other kind of transport or holiday tour that has been taken over by horrors! Ghost Airlines, Vampire Holidays, Zombie Tours – just let your imagination run riot:

Down at the Hotel Dread
the vampires are taking a break,
no vegetarian meals served here,
just tender and juicy steak.
No garlic in the goulash,
no glimpse of summer sun,
just Dracula on the TV
and vampires having fun!

"The north face" (p. 22)

In this poem I have used the image of a mountain's icy north face to describe the cold, unsmiling face of a rather grim teacher. When you use one thing to describe another it is called a metaphor. Sometimes you come across a metaphor in just one line of a poem, but here I've used it from the beginning of the poem right to the very end. Perhaps you can pick out the parts of the metaphor you think have worked well, and those which you think are not so good.

"Windy playground" (p. 25) and "Distributing the harvest" (p. 26)

Get into a group with a few friends and talk about these poems. Read them first, then pick out parts that you like or which you think sound unusual or special. What is it that's special about them? Are there parts of the poems that don't work for you? What do you think is wrong with them?

"Windy playground" was written on a very blustery day. Try picking out the words which show how strong the wind is.

In "Distributing the harvest" I've used something called alliteration. This is when sounds at the beginning of words are repeated a few times, like in the fifth line – "*b*allast the *b*ase of *b*askets". Alliteration is a very old device and is often used in poetry because it can help a poem sound stronger and more interesting to the ear. Can you find any other examples of alliteration in this poem? Try using alliteration in a line or two yourself.

"Whale" (p. 29)

What other creatures might you find in the museum of the future? What animals are facing extinction today? "In this room you will see an elephant . . ." – or a tiger, rhinoceros, polar bear, panda, and so on.

With a friend, discuss the animals you feel are in danger and together choose one to write about. First of all, make some notes. Think of words and phrases that describe the animal on one half of a piece of paper, and then on the other half, jot down any reasons you know for the animal's decline. Can the items in the second list be linked to those in the first list? For example, in the case of the tiger, you may come up with some good words or phrases about its wonderful striped coat for the first column, while in the second you could note that it's because of their skins that many tigers have been killed. When you've completed this stage, see whether the two lists will come together in a poem:

> There are no tigers to be seen any more
> but in this room we have the next best thing,
> a wonderfully preserved tiger skin.
> Just look at the markings,
> feel the texture,
> imagine the shooting party
> that slew this beast . . .

You could join up with others in your class to produce a book of poems about the extinct animals in the museum. It could be a guide to the exhibits.

"Fishing summer" (p. 34)
and "Knock down ginger" (p. 36)

These poems describe games and activities I enjoyed as a
child. What games do you play with friends? What are the
things you like to do when you're at home at weekends or
in the holidays? You may not think you do anything very
exciting – going to the pool with a friend, playing games in
the street – but when it comes to writing, it's usually better
to describe things you've actually done than make up things
you haven't. There are bound to be one or two memories
tucked away that will add colour and interest to what you
write. In "Fishing summer", for instance, I've tried to
achieve this with the bits about the old crab and "monster
congers"!

Have a go at jotting down ideas about a favourite activity.
You could do this on your own or with a friend. Dig deep
into your memory. Can you come up with something funny
or odd that you remember happening – or some of the
sights, smells and sounds you associate with that activity?

What sort of pattern is your poem going to have? You will
have noticed that poems have different rhythms and shapes,
depending on how long the lines are, whether they rhyme or
not, and so on. In "Fishing summer", I counted all the
syllables in every line. Syllables are the number of different
sounds a word makes when you say it; for example, the
word "fish-ing" has two syllables in it, and "sad-dle-bags"
has three. Every line in "Fishing summer" has ten syllables
in it. Count them if you don't believe me!

    Man-dy and I were fish-ing comp-an-ions
    rush-ing to catch the tide be-fore it turned.

I feel this has given the poem an interesting sound – an
intriguing rhythm.

Try counting the syllables in your poem. You need to start the pattern in the very first line, and then carry on from there. You don't have to use ten syllables, and you don't even have to use the same number of syllables in every line. You could build up a pattern of ten syllables in one line and then eight in the next, all the way through the poem. Whatever pattern you choose, though, keep it regular.

"Readathon-sleepathon" (p. 40)

I like fooling around with rhyme, and when I saw the words "Readathon-sleepathon" I just knew that I would have to extend this rhyme to take in other words. The trigger for this sort of wordplay doesn't have to be something extraordinary; sometimes it can just be something people say:

Don't be such a fusspot
an always-in-a-rushpot.

Don't be such a weepypot,
a sneak-to-Mum-and-be-creepypot.

Don't be such a . . .

You could play with words that you just like the sound of:

I was gob-smacked,
    shin-whacked,

    gift-wrapped,
    toe-tapped,

    guilt-wracked,
    hijacked . . .

Look for the rest of "Don't be such a fusspot . . ." and other poems that use language in a playful way in *My First Has Gone Bonkers*, an anthology of poems to puzzle over, edited by Brian Moses (Blackie).

"The cowpat-throwing contest" (p. 42)

Can you think of some other kind of contest that could
become the subject for a story poem – The World Record
Tree Climbing Contest, The Great Snail Race, The
Incredible Spaghetti Eating Competition, or something else?

> The World Record Tree Climbing Contest
> was taking place today,
> but Malc and me and Ian Grey,
> we climbed it last night,
> though we didn't say,
> just left a message pinned to the top:
> "Ran out of tree
> so we had to stop."
>
> Then later on, with the contest begun,
> we sat around to watch the fun, while
> fit-looking climbers were kitted up . . .

"Kiss chase" (p. 45)

I believe that some of the best writing can come out of
things people have felt or seen or done in their own lives.
Writing about how someone else might feel can also be
interesting, and may even help you see through someone
else's eyes – a very difficult thing to do.

If you are a boy, try writing about an activity that the girls
you know seem to enjoy. Try to imagine it from their point
of view.

If you are a girl, write about something that you know boys
enjoy doing. What is it they like about it? Can you see it
through their eyes?

I wonder how close you can get to saying something that
someone else really feels.